ELIJAH HARPER

POLITICIAN, PEACEMAKER & PIONEER OF THE OJI-CREE TRIBE | CANADIAN HISTORY FOR KIDS

True Canadian Heroes – Indigenous People of Canada Edition

www.ProfessorBeaver.ca

Print Edition: 9780228235224
Digital Edition: 9780228235231
Hardcover Edition: 9780228235842

Published by Speedy Publishing Canada Limited

PROFESSOR
BEAVER
Building Smarter and Brighter Minds

CONTENTS

QUICK FACTS ABOUT ELIJAH HARPER

Elijah Harper was a
politician, policy analyst
and a consultant.

Elijah Harper was a famous Oji-Cree Canadian. He was born on Red Sucker Lake Reserve, Manitoba on March 3, 1949. In addition to being a politician, he served as a policy analyst and a consultant.

DID YOU KNOW?

A policy analyst is someone who helps governments develop rules for what they do. The policy analyst does research on how the government's actions affect people and then gives advice.

Harper played a very critical part in preventing the Meech Lake Accord.

Harper is also well known for his humanitarian efforts (work that is done to improve people's lives or conditions) and his unfailing devotion to having the rights and roles of Indigenous people upheld. He played a very critical part in preventing the Meech Lake Accord.

DID YOU KNOW?

An accord is an official agreement that is reached between at least two people or groups of people.

It was Harper's refusal to agree to the content of the Meech Lake Accord that resulted in the Manitoba Legislature failing to meet the required deadline in having the accord approved.

Throughout his lifetime, Harper was given many honours and awards. He died on May 17, 2013 of heart failure that occurred from complications of diabetes.

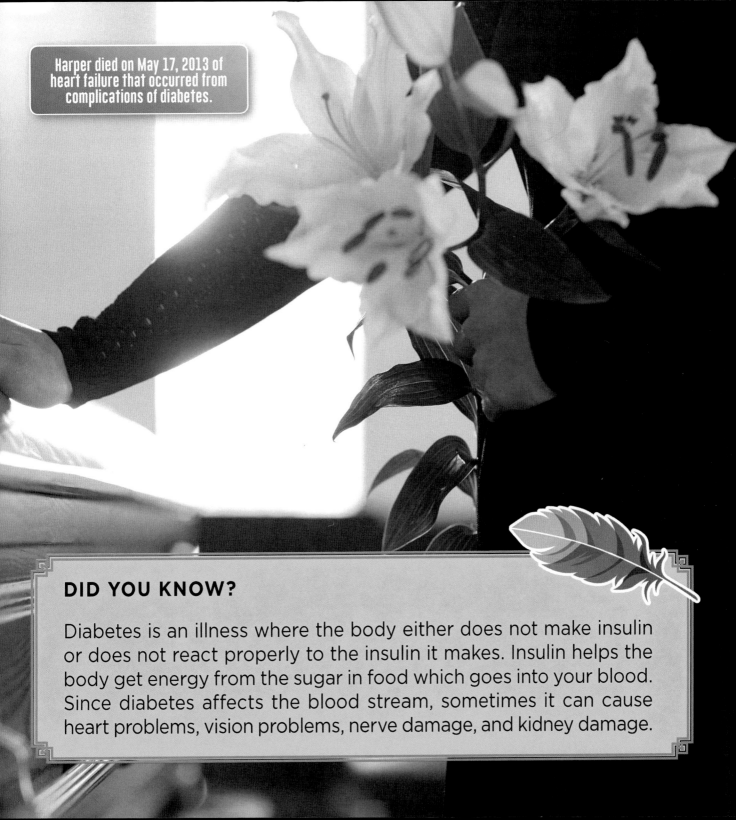

Harper died on May 17, 2013 of heart failure that occurred from complications of diabetes.

DID YOU KNOW?

Diabetes is an illness where the body either does not make insulin or does not react properly to the insulin it makes. Insulin helps the body get energy from the sugar in food which goes into your blood. Since diabetes affects the blood stream, sometimes it can cause heart problems, vision problems, nerve damage, and kidney damage.

THE EARLY DAYS OF ELIJAH HARPER

A view of part of the community and airport of Red Sucker Lake Reserve

lijah Harper was the son of Allan and Ethel Harper. He was born on March 3, 1949 on the Red Sucker Lake Reserve, in northeast Manitoba.

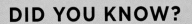

DID YOU KNOW?

A reserve is an area where Indigenous people live together in a community. The reserve where Elijah Harper was born is home to the Oji-Cree People.

The reserve where Harper was born is home to the Oji-Cree People.

For the first part of his childhood, Harper spent a lot of time with his grandfather who taught him great skills in fishing and hunting. One day, Harper was forced to leave his family home. Like many other Indigenous children in those days, he was sent to receive an education at a residential school.

Harper spent a lot of time with his grandfather who taught him great skills in fishing and hunting.

DID YOU KNOW?

Residential schools were places where Indigenous children were forced to be taught the European culture and ways of doing things.

The Norway House Residential School in Brandon

Students in a class at a residential school

Like many of his friends, Harper did not like being forced to abandon his own language and culture. Many children tried to run away from the residential schools, but they were caught and brought back.

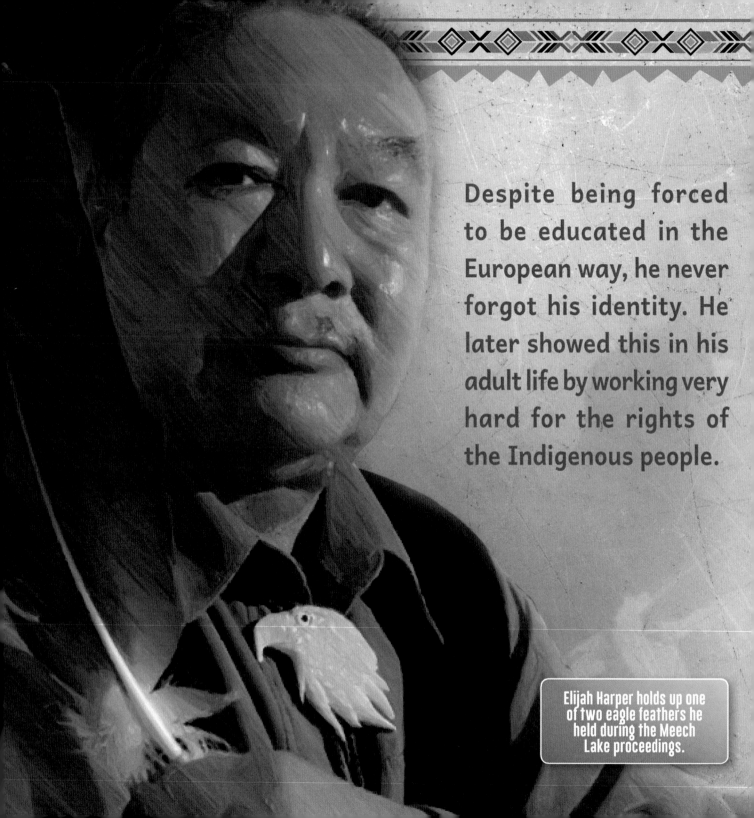

Despite being forced to be educated in the European way, he never forgot his identity. He later showed this in his adult life by working very hard for the rights of the Indigenous people.

Elijah Harper holds up one of two eagle feathers he held during the Meech Lake proceedings.

Through hard work and dedication, he rose to a position of government in which he could make a difference.

DID YOU KNOW?

There are many different groups of Cree and they have lived for millennia, (more than one thousand years), in the geographical area that goes from Alberta to Quebec. The Oji-Cree People, of whom Elijah Harper was a member, settled in parts of Manitoba and Ontario. They share a combined Cree and Ojibwa background.

Over the years, Harper went to different schools: Norway House, Brandon, Birtle, Garden Hill and Winnipeg, all of which are in the province of Manitoba.

Birtle Residential School
Manitoba, Canada

UNIVERSITY OF MA

The University of Manitoba

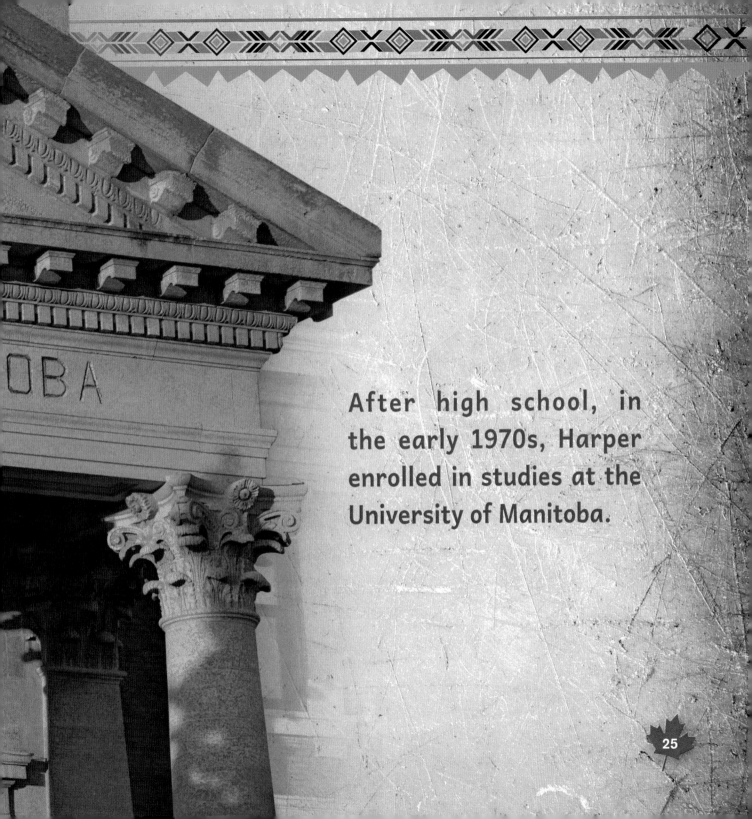

After high school, in the early 1970s, Harper enrolled in studies at the University of Manitoba.

After studying at the University of Manitoba for a couple years, he got a job as a community development worker. He did research and held the role of supervisor for the Manitoba Indian Brotherhood.

A token commemorating the 10th Anniversary of the Manitoba Indian Brotherhood

MANITOBA INDIAN BROTHER...

INDIAN TREATY No.6

1876

TENTH ANNIVERSARY

Terrasses de la Chaudiere houses the department headquarters of the Indigenous Northern Affairs in Gatineau, Quebec.

In addition, he became a program analyst for the Department of Northern Affairs for the province of Manitoba.

DID YOU KNOW?

Winnipeg is the capital city of the province of Manitoba and it is also the largest city in the province. The capital city is where the government is located, so the capital of a province is where the provincial government is found.

In 1978, Harper accepted the elected office of the Chief of the Red Sucker Lake Indian Band, which is now known as the Red Sucker Lake First Nation.

Harper accepted the elected office of the Chief of the Red Sucker Lake Indian Band.

DID YOU KNOW?

An elected office is the job that a person receives when they get the most people to vote for them instead of anybody else.

ELIJAH HARPER'S INVOLVEMENT IN PROVINCIAL POLITICS

Harper is known for being the first Indigenous person to be elected as a Member of the Legislative Assembly (MLA) in the province of Manitoba.

34

DID YOU KNOW?

A legislative assembly is a group of people who have been elected to work in their province or territory to make laws. A member of the legislative assembly is a person who is voted in by the people to represent them. The member can vote to pass or change a law.

One of the hallways inside the legislative building of Manitoba

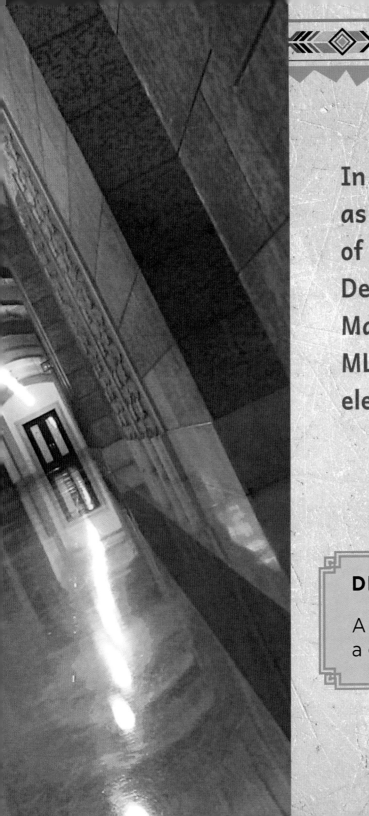

In 1981, Harper won a seat as MLA for the constituency of Rupertsland for the New Democratic Party (NDP) in Manitoba. Harper served as MLA for his constituency for eleven years.

DID YOU KNOW?

A constituency is an area in which a group of voters live.

In 1986, he received an important appointment. He was the person who was designated to cabinet to serve as Minister Without Portfolio for Native Affairs.

DID YOU KNOW?

A Cabinet is a group of people who carry out regular duties of a government.

Harper was designated to cabinet to serve as Minister Without Portfolio for Native Affairs

After becoming involved in a motor vehicle accident in September, 1987, in which alcohol was involved, Harper was no longer able to keep this position. However, he realized the consequences of his actions. He entered rehabilitation, (the official help and training a person receives to overcome an illness or damaging habit.)

He never drank alcohol again. He was given back the position as Minister of Native affairs. After that, in November 1987, he became the Minister of Northern Affairs.

DID YOU KNOW?

A minister is the head of a government office. In Canada, the Prime Minister is the person who is the head of the federal government.

Harper was involved in a motor vehicle accident in which alcohol was involved.

ELIJAH HARPER'S INFLUENCE ON THE OUTCOME OF THE MEECH LAKE ACCORD

The Government Conference Centre in Ottawa, where all signing ceremonies with regard to the Accord were held

One of the reasons Harper became so well known across Canada, was the way in which he prevented the Meech Lake Accord from going ahead. The purpose of the Meech Lake Accord was to make amendments (changes) to the Canadian Constitution.

DID YOU KNOW?

A constitution is a list of basic principles that a country or group of people use to govern themselves.

Quebec, Canada

One focus of the Meech Lake Accord was to recognize Quebec as a distinct society. Harper did not disagree with that at all. However, he wanted to make sure that the rights and roles of the Indigenous Peoples were also kept.

He believed that just as the French culture and language should be recognized, the cultures and languages of members of the Indigenous Peoples of Canada should also be protected. For the amendments to be made to the constitution, every MLA had to say "yes" to the accord.

Harper believed that the culture and language of members of the Indigenous Peoples of Canada should be protected.

However, when it was Harper's turn to cast his vote, he refused to agree because in addition to the rights of the English and the French, he wanted to make sure that Indigenous People also had rights. On eight separate times, while raising an eagle feather, he very calmly and politely refused to say 'yes' because the Indigenous People had not been included or recognized.

As a result, the deadline to vote on the Meech Lake Accord passed, which resulted in the accord never being approved.

Harper raising an eagle feather

THE CANADIAN PRESS
Canada's trusted news leader

In 1990, Harper was recognized several times. His determination had paid off! He was voted 'Newsmaker of the year' by the Canadian Press for his refusal to agree with the Meech Lake Accord.

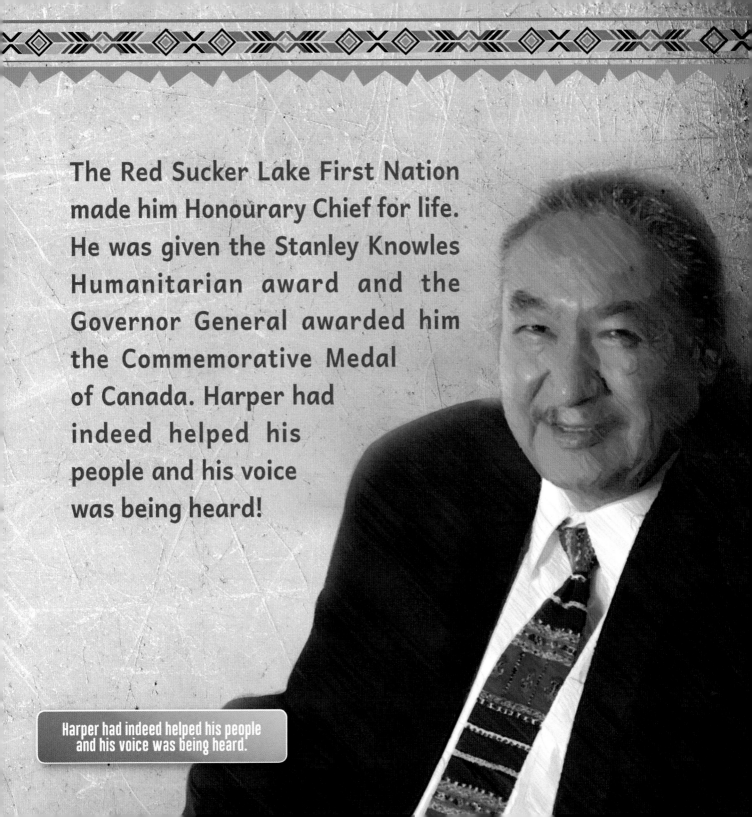

The Red Sucker Lake First Nation made him Honourary Chief for life. He was given the Stanley Knowles Humanitarian award and the Governor General awarded him the Commemorative Medal of Canada. Harper had indeed helped his people and his voice was being heard!

Harper had indeed helped his people and his voice was being heard.

ELIJAH HARPER'S INTERNATIONAL ROLES

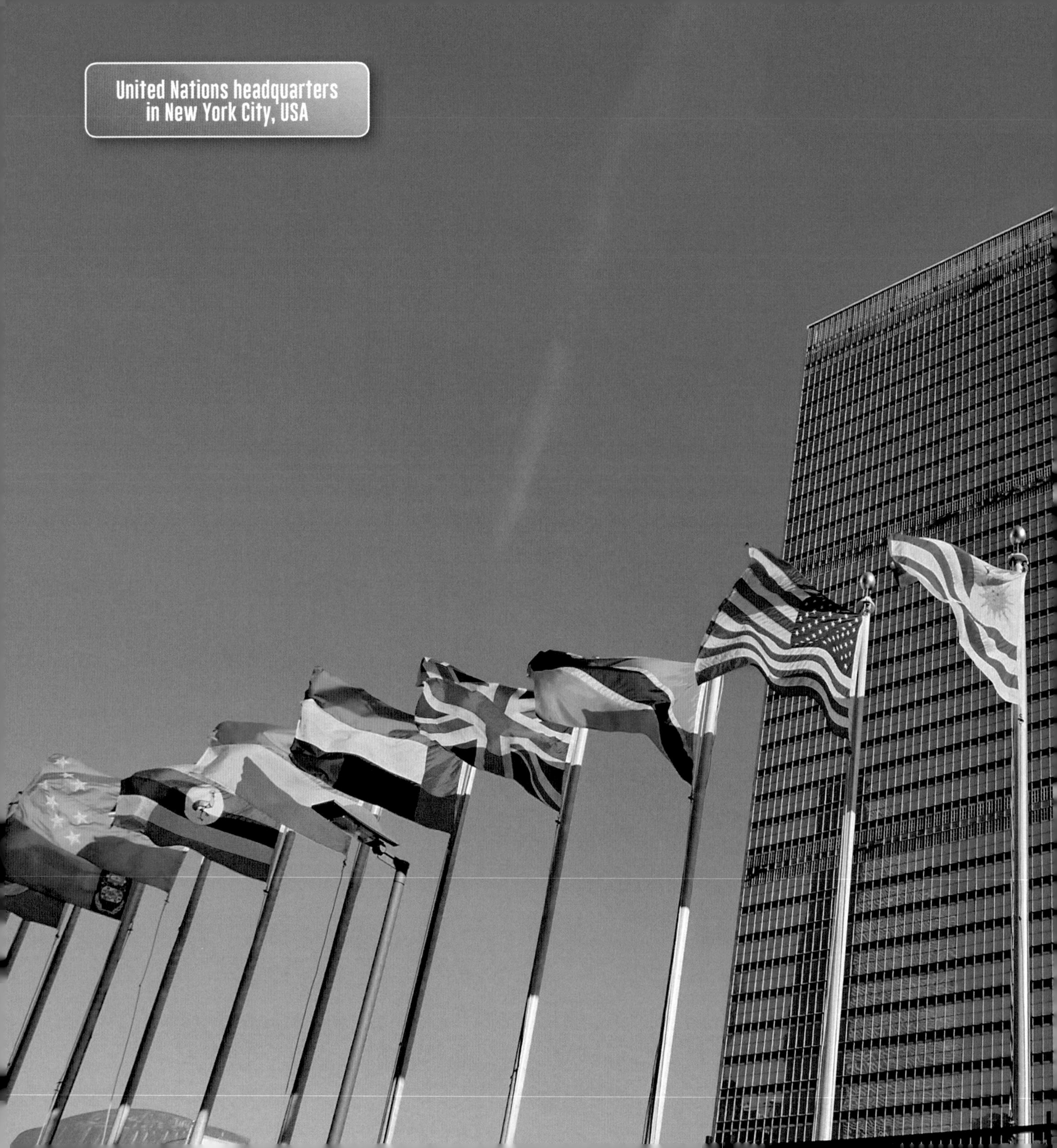

United Nations headquarters in New York City, USA

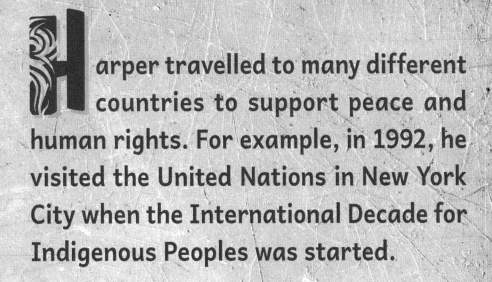

Harper travelled to many different countries to support peace and human rights. For example, in 1992, he visited the United Nations in New York City when the International Decade for Indigenous Peoples was started.

DID YOU KNOW?

The United Nations (UN) replaced the League of Nations after World War Two (WWII). The UN is an international organization that tries to promote peace and cooperation between nations and to improve the quality of human life.

Harper later returned to New York City to witness the Declaration of International Indigenous Day. In addition to his travels to many countries, his political and peaceful interests took him to the Hague.

DID YOU KNOW?

Not only is the Hague the city where the main government of the Netherlands, in Europe, is located, it is the place where the International Court of Justice is found.

The Hague is a city in The Netherlands.

Harper participated in overseas humanitarian work through World Vision.

His work was not only focused on politics and giving speeches. He also participated in overseas humanitarian work through World Vision.

DID YOU KNOW?

World Vision is a Christian charity that helps bring relief and help to people to fight poverty and unfair treatment.

ELIJAH HARPER'S INVOLVEMENT IN FEDERAL POLITICS

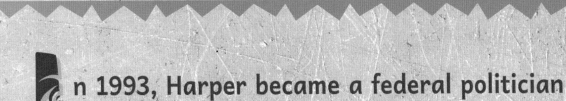

n 1993, Harper became a federal politician for the Liberal Party.

Harper was voted in as a Member of Parliament (MP) for the Churchill constituency in northern Manitoba. He held this job until 1997. Elijah Harper worked very hard for recognition of the Indigenous People.

DID YOU KNOW?

In Canada, a federal politician works at the nation's capital, Ottawa, and Parliament is the federal legislature. Federal means the government that unites all the provinces and territories of Canada.

St. Paul University in Ottawa

In 1996, he was given the National Aboriginal Achievement Award. Not only did Harper respect and promote the rights of the Indigenous People, he also promoted peace among all people. He was bestowed the Award of Merit from the Canadian Institute for Conflict Resolution (CICR), a partner of Saint Paul University, in 1998.

Harper was also known for his contributions to bringing peace and harmony among different groups of people across Canada. In the interests of peace, he urged that both Indigenous and non-Indigenous come together for a Sacred Assembly for spiritual healing and reconciliation (bringing people together in a friendly way).

In December 1995, in Hull, Quebec, during the meeting of the Sacred Assembly, there were apologies made for the cultural harm that had been inflicted on the Indigenous people.

Moreover, National Aboriginal Day was established, and it is observed on June 21st. Later, the Privy Council made Elijah Harper a commissioner of the Indian Claims Commission.

DID YOU KNOW?

The Privy Council is a group of people chosen to advise and give help to the Prime Minister. The group helps organize and coordinate various government offices.

onal Aboriginal
ny Celebration

National Aboriginal Day is
observed on June 21st

He accepted this appointment in 1999. He worked very hard in this role until he resigned in 2000. Nonetheless, he still accepted many speaking engagements until he passed away.

DID YOU KNOW?

A commissioner is someone put in charge of a commission. A commission is a group of people who are given something specific to do, in this case to look after Indian Claims.

Harper accepted many speaking engagements until he passed away.

ELIJAH HARPER'S DEATH

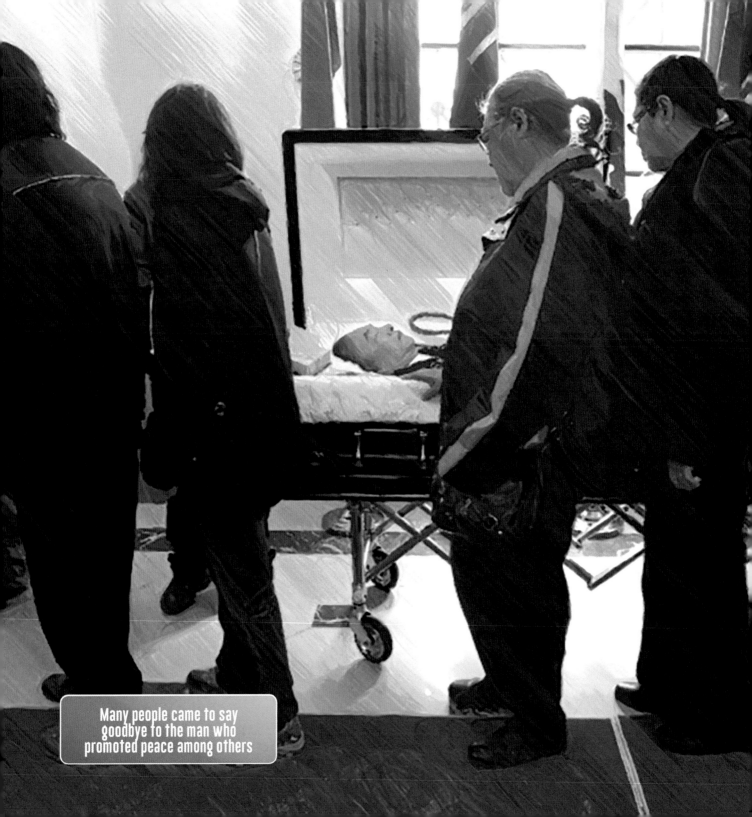

Many people came to say goodbye to the man who promoted peace among others

Elijah Harper died in Ottawa, the capital city of Canada, on May 17, 2013. His heart stopped beating because of problems from diabetes. He was sixty-four years old. His remains were sent back to the provincial legislature of Manitoba.

Many people came to say goodbye to the man who not only did so much to promote and uphold the rights and roles of the Indigenous People, but who also promoted peace among others. After a funeral service in Winnipeg, Harper's body was sent back to Red Sucker Lake First Nation for burial.

Both the University of Manitoba
and Carleton University gave
Harper Honourary Doctor of Laws

It is no wonder that, just three years before his death, he was presented with the Order of Manitoba, an award that is bestowed on someone who has made outstanding contributions.

Both the University of Manitoba and Carleton University gave him Honourary Doctor of Laws. Indeed, he was an inspiration to many people, and can be considered a true Canadian hero!

Manufactured by Amazon.ca
Bolton, ON